iCONLOGiC ™

Version: 120723
Page Count: 80
9781960604170 (KDP)
9781960604187 (eBook/Kindle)

Training Materials, Presentations, and U.S. Copyright Law

Avoid copyright infringement with this no-nonsense, plain language guide.

Kevin Siegel
Linda Wolf Rohrbaugh

Contents

About the Authors

Kevin Siegel is the founder and president of IconLogic, Inc. He has authored and published hundreds books on subjects such as Adobe Captivate, TechSmith Camtasia, Articulate Storyline, Articulate Rise, iSpring Suite, Adobe RoboHelp, Adobe Presenter, Adobe Technical Communication Suite, and CenarioVR.

Kevin spent five years in the U.S. Coast Guard as an award-winning photojournalist and has three decades of experience as a print publisher, technical writer, instructional designer, and eLearning developer. He is a certified technical trainer, a veteran classroom instructor, and a frequent speaker at trade shows and conventions. He is also a Certified Online Training Professional (COTP) with the International Council for Certified Online Training Professionals (ICCOTP). You can reach Kevin at ksiegel@iconlogic.com.

Linda Wolff Rohrbaugh is an attorney who advises businesses, freelancers, and nonprofits concerning practical matters of business and intellectual property law and compliance. She worked in the publishing field for over a decade and has over a decade of experience teaching law to university and law school students. Linda holds multiple professional certifications, including the International Association of Privacy Professionals CIPP/US and CIPM designations. She has written numerous books and manuals for regulated professions. Additionally, she is the author of the upcoming book: *Essential Law for Independent Businesses*.

What is Copyright?

According to U.S. Copyright Office (copyright.gov), and in the book *Copyright Law of the United States (Title 17),* "Copyright is a type of intellectual property that protects original works of authorship as soon as an author fixes the work in a tangible form of expression."

Many types of works can be protected by copyright, including, but not limited to:

- Paintings

- Photographs

- Illustrations

- Musical Compositions

- Sound Recordings

- Computer Programs

- Books

- Poems

- Blog Posts

- Movies

- Architectural Works

- Plays

Once you own a copyright, you can allow other people to use it. You can also prevent other people from using your copyright. Furthermore, you can sell your entire copyright, or only a portion of it.

You can download a free PDF of the *Copyright Law of the United States (Title 17)* book mentioned earlier from https://www.copyright.gov/title17/.

Although the book contains nearly 500 pages, is loaded with legal jargon, and isn't necessarily entertaining or easy to read, it is a great reference to add to your library.

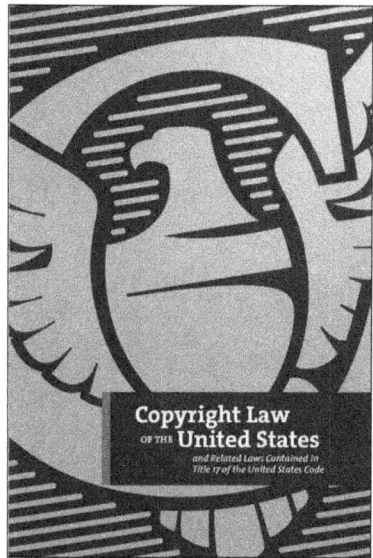

Copyright Law
OF THE **United States**
and Related Laws Contained in
Title 17 of the United States Code

Works that are considered authored

Later in this book, we will cover the categories of authored works in detail. Generally speaking, a work is considered authored if it's original and is fixed in a tangible medium. Let's delve more into what that means.

Originality

A work must be original for it to be copyrightable. In the copyright world, the word original has a precise meaning. Furthermore, the work must contain enough creative elements to be considered creative. We've used the word creative twice, but that's how copyright works. To be considered copyrightable, the work must have a fraction of creativity or originality.

For example, Bob creates a rectangle in Microsoft PowerPoint.

The rectangle Bob created is shown below. (Note that if you are listening to the audio edition of this book, all figures and illustrations mentioned are included in your companion PDF.)

Figure 1: Bob's rectangle.

A rectangle is a common symbol. While Bob's rectangle is fine, there isn't enough creativity to warrant a copyright.

Here's another example:

Jennie draws some characters to use in her eLearning storyboard. Her illustrations appear in the image shown below.

Sample Storyboard for Office Etiquette		
Lesson Name: Welcoming a Client to the Office		
Slide #	Screen	Voiceover
1)		Don't let social awkwardness keep you from making a good first impression on your client. When a client comes to your office, you'll want to make sure to put them at their ease. Knowing the social niceties and having a plan will help you welcome a guest to your office with confidence. That will put your mind at ease, too!

Figure 2: Jennie's stick figure characters.

While common shapes, such as Bob's rectangle, cannot be copyrighted, Jennie feels that her stick figure illustrations are original works of art. The images can be copyrighted, correct?

Stick figures may be eligible for a copyright if they are original enough. However, Jennie's figures lack originality so they cannot be copyrighted.

How Long Does a Copyright Last?

When it comes to copyright duration, it depends on whether a human or a company created the content.

If a human created the content, the copyright lasts for a lifetime plus 70 years. If you collaborate with co-authors, the 70-year duration begins the day the last author dies.

A company's copyright would not be life plus 70 years because a company's longevity is not comparable to human years. Instead, it would be either 95 or 120 years, depending on whether or not the work has been distributed to the public.

What Rights Do You Get With a Copyright?

Once you have obtained a copyright, you have the following rights to your work.

- You have the right to control copies of the work.

- You have the right to control distribution of the work.

- You have the right to control the adaptation of the work.

- And you have the right to control public performance or display of the work.

Is It Necessary to File for a Copyright?

Alana writes a training book for an upcoming class. She adds the following text to the footer of every page in the book: © **2024, Alana**.

In addition to putting the copyright notice in the book, does Alana need to file for the copyright to protect her authorship rights?

The answer is, no. The instant Alana saved the file for her book, it was automatically protected by copyright.

If Alana does add a copyright notice to the book, she does get one specific benefit in the United States: people reading the book cannot claim the "innocent infringer defense." Sure, an infringer can claim that they were unaware that the book was protected by copyright. However, that defense won't work.

The "I didn't know" defense is similar to arguing against a speeding ticket by telling the police officer that you didn't see the posted speed limit sign or didn't know the speed limit.

Speaking of the copyright notice, we mentioned that Alana added the copyright notice to the footer of every book page. Did she need to go to that extreme?

No, she did not. However, the copyright notice must be placed in a logical location. For instance, adding the copyright notice on the title page of each module would work nicely.

Artificial Intelligence and Copyright

If you've ever used **ChatGPT** or AI image creation tools such as Adobe Firefly, you know just how easy it is to create content.

AI Content and Copyright

ChatGPT (https://openai.com/chatgpt) was asked the following: "I am writing a book about copyright law related to training materials and presentations. What are the most important things readers should know about copyright?"

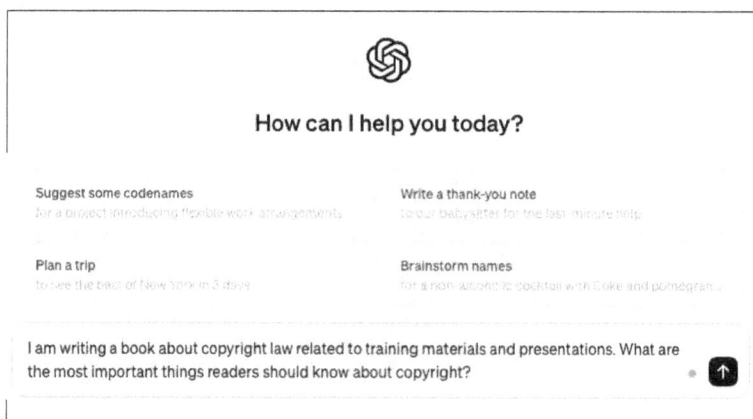

How can I help you today?

Suggest some codenames
for a project introducing flexible work arrangements.

Write a thank-you note
to our babysitter for the last-minute help.

Plan a trip
to see the best of New York in 3 days.

Brainstorm names
for a non-alcoholic cocktail with Coke and pomegran...

I am writing a book about copyright law related to training materials and presentations. What are the most important things readers should know about copyright?

Figure 3: ChatGPT prompt for what to include in a book about copyright law.

In seconds, ChatGPT returned some beneficial information. The information given by ChatGPT is quoted verbatim below. **Note that the copyright for this book does not protect the following information because it came directly from ChatGPT.**

"In the context of copyright law related to training materials and presentations, one of the most important things to understand is that copyright protection applies automatically when original works are created. Here are vital points that authors, trainers, and presenters should be aware of:

Automatic Protection: Copyright protection is automatic upon the creation of original works, including training materials and presentations. It is not necessary to register the work with a copyright office although registration can provide additional benefits.

Exclusive Rights: Copyright grants the creator exclusive rights to reproduce, distribute, perform, display, and create derivative works based on their original work. This means others cannot use, reproduce, or distribute the materials without permission.

Fair Use: While copyright grants exclusive rights to creators, there are limitations, such as 'fair use.' Fair use allows for the limited use of copyrighted material for purposes such as criticism, commentary, news reporting, teaching, scholarship, and research. However, determining fair use is subjective and depends on various factors.

Permission and Licensing: To use someone else's copyrighted material, it's crucial to obtain permission or a license. This is especially important for training materials and presentations where using third-party content may be common.

Work for Hire: If training materials and/or presentations are created as part of employment or under a contract specifying 'work for hire,' the employer or contracting party may own the copyright rather than the individual creator.

Creative Commons and Open Source Licensing: Some creators choose to license their works under

Creative Commons or open source licenses, allowing others to use the materials under certain conditions. It's important to understand the terms of such licenses.

Duration of Copyright: Copyright protection is not unlimited. The duration of copyright protection varies by jurisdiction, but it typically lasts for the life of the author plus a certain number of years (e.g., 70 years in many countries).

Digital Millennium Copyright Act (DMCA): The DMCA provides a framework for addressing online copyright infringement issues, including procedures for taking down infringing content and addressing disputes.

Keep Records: It's wise to keep records of when the work was created, who the authors are, and any permissions or licenses obtained. This documentation can be crucial in case of copyright disputes.

Stay Informed: Copyright laws and regulations may change, so it's essential to stay informed about developments in copyright law that may impact the use and protection of training materials and presentations.

Consulting with a legal professional specializing in intellectual property law is also advisable to ensure compliance with copyright laws and to address specific situations that may arise in the context of training materials and presentations."

Artificial Intelligence (AI) is not human, so under current laws, rules, regulations, and copyright guides, AI output cannot be protected by copyright.

Substantial original material must be added to the AI content for it to receive copyright protection for something created using AI.

However, if you change the AI content enough and add your creative material, you can at least own a copyright on the original material.

These days, people use AI to write anything from quizzes to books to screenplays. While the quality of the writing in the AI is usually fine, it is a bit of a mystery to find out where that content comes from.

AI Quizzes and Copyright

Here's an example of how AI content can cause trouble: ChatGPT was prompted to write five multiple-choice questions about Articulate Storyline 360. The quiz was to have one correct answer and three distractors. (Note that Storyline 360 is a popular eLearning development tool.)

write five multiple-choice questions about Articulate Storyline 360 with one correct answer and three distractors

Figure 4: The prompt in ChatGPT to write give multiple-choice questions about Storyline.

Here is what ChatGPT created in a few seconds:

Question 1: What is the primary purpose of Articulate Storyline 360?

A) Video Editing

B) Animation Creation

C) E-Learning Course Development

D) Graphic Design

Question 2: Which feature in Articulate Storyline 360 allows for responsive design in e-learning courses?

A) Slide Transitions

B) Drag-and-Drop Interactions

C) Fluid Box

D) Animation Effects

Question 3: What is the purpose of the "States" feature in Articulate Storyline 360?

A) Managing Layers

B) Customizing Object Appearance

C) Audio Editing

D) Importing External Media

Question 4: Which publishing format is NOT supported by Articulate Storyline 360?

A) SCORM

B) HTML5

C) PDF

D) Tin Can API (xAPI)

Question 5: What is the function of the "Triggers" panel in Articulate Storyline 360?

A) Managing Slide Transitions

B) Controlling Object Actions and Events

C) Adjusting Audio Levels

D) Inserting Stock Images

At first glance, the quiz looks fine. However, upon closer inspection, **question 2** is a problem. ChatGPT lists Fluid Box as the correct answer. However, Storyline does not currently offer a Fluid Box feature at all.

When creating quiz questions, ensure your quiz content is legally defensible. If your exam included this question and answer, you could be held responsible for not only the quiz content but also the pass/fail status of the learner, who could argue that your quiz was unfair because it contained incorrect or misleading content.

AI and Image Copyright

As with AI text, images created with AI are not protected by copyright law.

Here's an example of an image created with Adobe Firefly (https://www.adobe.com/sensei/generative-ai/firefly.html).

There is a field in Firefly where you can ask for almost anything. In this example, Firefly was prompted to create an image of a **mouse holding a copyright symbol.**

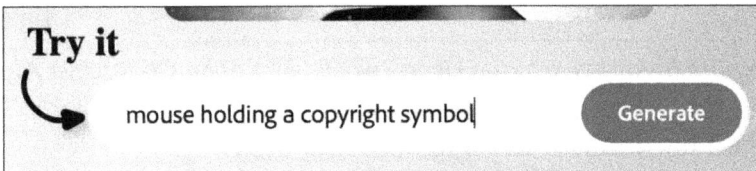

Figure 5: A prompt to create an image in Firefly AI.

Before Firefly created the image, a prompt appeared displaying the User Guidelines. The user must agree to the guidelines before proceeding.

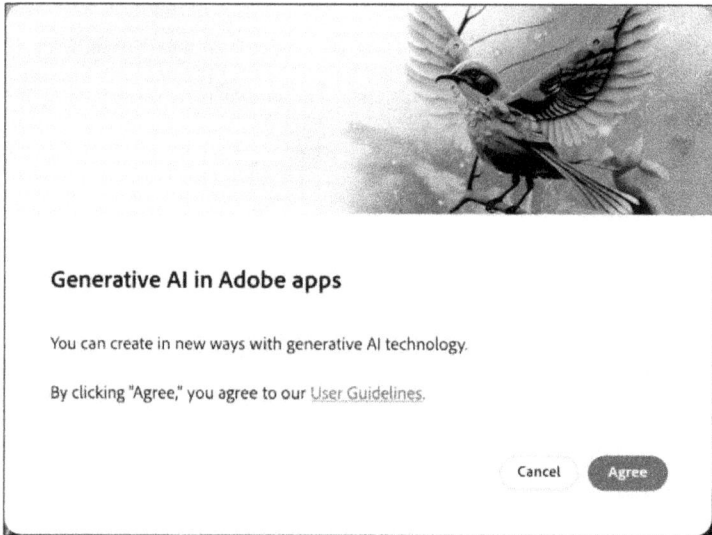

Generative AI in Adobe apps

You can create in new ways with generative AI technology.

By clicking "Agree," you agree to our User Guidelines.

Cancel   Agree

Figure 6: Agreeing to the User Guidelines, Adobe Generative AI.

And here is where things can get tricky.

Have you read the user guidelines? If you have read the guidelines, do you truly understand them?

If you return and create another image a month from now, the guidelines might have changed. Have you re-read the guidelines and are you aware of what has changed?

If you're curious about what Firefly created based upon the "mouse holding a copyright symbol" prompt, here's the image. It was generated and appeared onscreen in less than 30 seconds.

Figure 7: An AI image of a mouse holding a copyright symbol.

Assuming the Firefly user guidelines allow you to use the image in your training or presentation, go ahead and move forward. Note, however, that you cannot receive a copyright for the AI-generated image.

Text-to-Speech Voices and Copyright

Text-to-speech, or AI Voices, is often used in eLearning as an alternative to human voiceover audio.

There are several advantages to using text-to-speech (TTS) instead of a human. For instance, TTS voices are typically less expensive than hiring voiceover talent. It's quicker to use TTS rather than relying on a human voice. This is because TTS audio quality is consistent compared to a human recording created outside a professional studio.

Here's a scenario involving an eLearning developer named Andi. She wants to include audio in the course and will use AI voices to fulfill that goal.

Andi can utilize any one of several AI voice providers to create her voiceover files, such as WellSaid Labs (https://wellsaidlabs.com), Amazon Polly (https://aws.amazon.com/polly/), or TTS agents within the eLearning tools themselves.

The process of creating TTS is simple. In most instances, the voiceover script text is selected, sentence by sentence, or paragraph by paragraph, and then a click of the "Create Audio" button completes the task.

In the image below, the process of creating TTS in Adobe Captivate is shown.

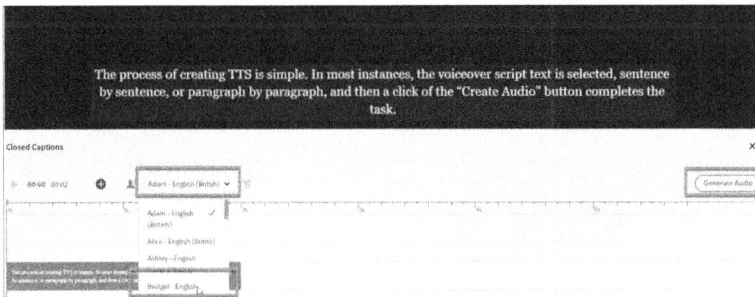

Figure 8: Creating TTS in Adobe Captivate 12, 2023 edition.

Relying on TTS in your training raises two copyright concerns:

1. Is the voiceover script used to create the TTS output copyrightable?

2. Who owns the audio file output by the TTS provider?

If Andi writes the script and she doesn't use AI, she owns the copyright to the script. Thus, the script is protected by copyright.

Ownership of the TTS audio files isn't so cut and dry.

Andi can use the TTS voices in her eLearning course subject to the license terms specified by the organization that owns the TTS technology.

In the example above, Andi used WellSaid labs and must understand the ownership limitations documented in the WellSaid license agreement.

What may be surprising to people who rely on AI voice is that they do not own the sound recordings created by the TTS technologies.

Suppose Andi is filing a registration with the copyright office. In that case, she must document that AI was used for the audio files, which would likely result in her copyright claim being denied.

Sharing Copyright

Laura and Joe decide to collaborate on a book. Without a written agreement specifying something different, Laura and Joe automatically own an equal percentage of the book's copyright.

Laura and Joe both have the right to use the book without obtaining permission from the other. However, because Laura and Joe share the copyright, book royalties will have to be shared equally.

A company can own a copyright if human employees create the content.

If Laura and Joe write a book on company time or using company equipment, the company owns the copyright to that book unless there is a signed agreement to the contrary.

Copyright Roles

There are three copyright roles: author, claimant, and exclusive rights holder.

The author is the individual who provides original content for the piece.

The claimant is the person who owns the actual copyright.

An author may be the original claimant but may also sell all or part of their copyright to someone else. That person now becomes a claimant who has rights to the work.

If you are an author and transfer your copyright to a publisher under a license agreement, the publisher holds your exclusive rights. The publisher can then file for the copyright.

How Do You File a Copyright?

Filing a copyright is easier and less expensive than you might imagine. If you file for a copyright yourself, it costs $65.

The $65 fee is for a single work, but you can create a group registration.

For example, if you have 750 photographs in your possession, you do not need to register them one at a time and pay $65 for each one. Instead, you can group them and then register each group one at a time. Registering a group will cost more than $65, but not much more than that.

Additionally, you can register 10 songs from an album in one registration. You can also register short stories altogether in one registration.

If you hire someone to file the copyright on your behalf, it will cost you more.

To file a copyright yourself, go to **https:// www.copyright.gov**.

Click **Registration > Register Your Work: Registration Portal**.

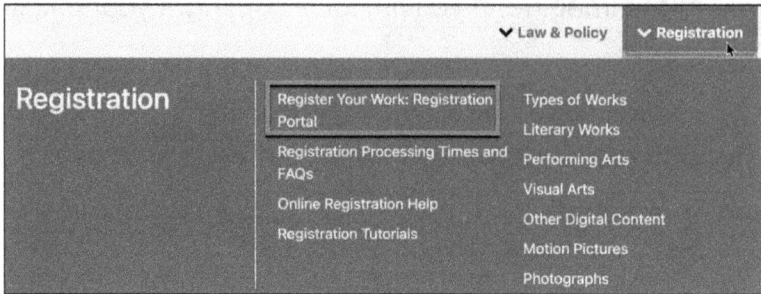

Figure 9: Register Your Work: Registration Portal.

Click **Log in to the Electronic Copyright Office (eCO) Registration System** button and create an account.

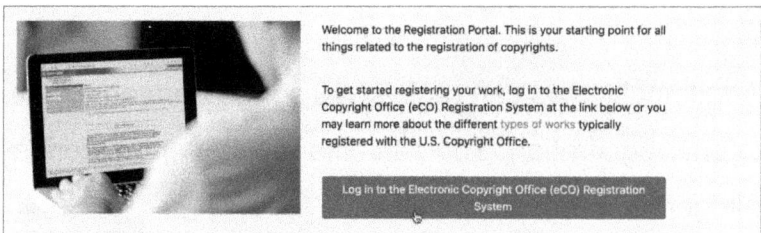

Figure 10: Log in to the Electronic Copyright Office (eCO) Registration System.

You will use the eCO Registration System to register, preregister, and upload digital copies of your work.

Applying for a copyright is a very different process compared to filing your work with organizations such as the Writer's Guild of America (WGA). If you're a writer and file with the WGA, that filing is not a copyright. The WGA notice simply alerts guild members about your book but offers no official copyright protection.

Why Should You File For a Copyright?

Earlier in this book, you learned that you do not have to file for copyright physically because copyright protections exist when you save your work.

Why bother spending the money or making the effort to file for a copyright? Are there any benefits to actually filing?

Spending the $65 copyright filing fee and completing the filing process is an insurance policy that will pay dividends if anybody copies or steals your work.

If an infringement occurs and you've already filed and registered the copyright, you can go to court and say, "I would like to get $30,000 for each violation of my copyright, please."

The court will likely agree with you if you've registered the copyright.

If you haven't registered the copyright before the infringement occurs, you must prove how much harm there was. If you are required to prove something in court, you will need to hire a lawyer, which can get expensive.

Remember that even if you win a copyright infringement case, there's no guarantee that you will collect enough money to justify the effort or expense.

If the other person did not make money off the copyright infringement, chances are you won't be able to prove damages.

Suppose you are notified that your copyright has been violated. Instead of hiring a lawyer or going to court, you can contact the infringer by writing and then sending a letter to them.   The letter should convey something along the lines of, "I'll let you continue doing what you're doing if you compensate me."

When Should You File For a Copyright?

Suppose you begin to write a book. As the book takes shape, you decide it's worth protecting. When should you file for a copyright? Should you file as you make each draft or wait until the book is finished?

Every version is going to be automatically covered by copyright. We recommend that you not spend a lot of money registering a bunch of initial drafts. Instead, wait until you have your work close to its final form and then file.

Later, if you revise your work with a second or third edition, you can file additional copyrights referencing the first copyright.

Fair Use

Fair use is the constitutional freedom of expression that says, as a country, we value the right to build upon creative works.

In the United States, citizens can reuse creative works in certain limited situations: for criticism, commentary, education, parody, and some other nonprofit-type considerations.

By claiming your constitutional right to fair use, you acknowledge that you have infringed on someone's copyright. You admit that you copied somebody else's work without consent and reused it. However, you believe that you have a good reason for the infringement.

If you end up in court, there are four factors that the court will use to determine whether it's fair use or infringement.

Purpose and character of the use

Why are you using copyrighted work? Are you just copying the original work or transforming it into something new? The more you change the work from its original version, the stronger your case for fair use.

Are you using copyrighted work for a commercial or noncommercial purpose? If you're trying to use copyrighted work to attract attention to a product, service, or cause, your goal may be seen as commercial. This strategy won't be considered defensible. If you're using work to make fun of it, teach about it, or criticize it for a noncommercial purpose, then it's more likely to be considered justifiable.

What kind of original work did you borrow?

Was the copyrighted work highly original or creative, like a song? Courts favor copyright protection of original and creative content.

Was the copyrighted work more factual, like a biography, documentary, or a news broadcast? These examples are going to be less protected.

How much did you use?

How much of the copyrighted material did you use, and how important was it to the work?

Using as little of the original piece as possible would be best. Keep in mind that it may be too much if that little bit is the heart of the work, the hook, or the "who did it."

Impact on the market

Finally, we look at the impact on the market for the original. If your use replaces any potential market for the original work, it will weigh against you.

In 1990, Vanilla Ice's song Ice Ice Baby copied the signature bassline from the song Under Pressure by Queen and David Bowie.

Ice argued that his melody was different from the one that was used in Under Pressure.

You can judge for yourself by watching this video on YouTube: **https://tinyurl.com/4hkvh627**.

Ice eventually claimed that his intended use of the melody in Ice Ice Baby was just a joke. The case was settled out of court for an undisclosed amount of money. In addition, David Bowie and the members of Queen received songwriting credit for Ice Ice Baby.

Can you use a portion of copyrighted music?

An eLearning developer used a portion of a well-known song in his course. When asked if he had permission to use the music, he said he'd been assured by legal "experts" that trainers can use up to 30 seconds, or 10%, of copyrighted music without worrying about copyright infringement.

What a great deal for trainers everywhere!

It turns out that the "expert" legal advice did not exist. The myth started with a group at a California university trying to set a standard where educators could use music in their training courses without fear of breaking copyright law.

The group's "standard" was never adopted by anyone, nor did any court ever support it.

To be clear, audio media is not free to use in your training. Whether with or without music, sound recordings are copyrightable and have a complex maze of protection.

There are two copyrights in a sound recording: one for the author and another for the recording artist/ producer. Both need to be cleared if an individual intends to use a recorded song or another audio piece. In addition, each copyright falls under different protection periods. If the author's rights have expired, the individual may still need clearance for the sound recording if it is still under copyright. Failing to obtain proper permission can result in a lawsuit for up to $150,000 per song or audio clip used, even if there wasn't a profit made off the work.

Audio performance rights are held by the audio's author (also known in music as the composer or songwriter) and apply to any performance of the notes, melodies, and words for people other than just close friends and family. It applies whether a cover song is being composed to post on social media for fun, or someone's recorded version is being used in an online course.

Authors may independently handle copyright release requests or may have given these rights to an agent such as a music publisher. There may even be multiple copyright owners and agents. It is vital to get consent from ALL of them just to be safe.

Music rights owners can be researched online using a database called **Songfile** (https://www.songfile.com).

Audio Use Strategies

Audio in the public domain can be freely reused, BUT (and this is a big caveat!) first, check the date the recording was made.

Any audio created before 1922 is okay. Of course, there won't be much variety because audio recordings weren't as easily accessible until the 1930s and 1940s.

If the audio was recorded after 1927, consent will be required from the recording artist/label to use the audio in one's own training.

It is also recommended to license a portion of the audio from the owner or agent.

Music libraries such as **Musicbed** (https://www.musicbed.com/) are excellent sources for various genres and lengths of original music clips. Pricing is determined by how the music will be put to use.

Another popular source for music is **Easy Song Licensing** (https://www.easysong.com). They include negotiated rates for some music. They can also negotiate on your behalf to get the rights to use clips that require independent licenses.

Of course, if you have the time, talent, and equipment, you can always record your audio and use it as you see fit. Furthermore, anything you create will be copyright-protected once you save the file.

Derivative Works

It's almost guaranteed that you have seen at least a portion of the show The Simpsons. The show started in 1989 and is currently the longest-running animated comedy in history.

Homer Simpson, one of the show's main characters, is famous for his catchphrase "D'oh!"

A tee-shirt designer wants to use the catchphrase on a new shirt but fears breaking copyright law. Instead of using "D'oh," she goes with "Dohhhh!" She claims that the extra letters make her version very different from the original; thus, her version is a derivative work. Because it's a derivative work, she will get around the copyright concerns.

True or False?

Homer's "Doh!" is too short to be considered original and creative enough to be copyrightable. So, that little phrase is not going to be a copyright problem. However, using the word on a tee-shirt could be a trademark issue, which is outside the scope of this book. The company that produces The Simpsons owns a trademark for the sound recording of Homer saying that sound, but they don't own a trademark for the actual word itself.

A young painter loves Leonardo da Vinci's painting of Mona Lisa and decides to make a parody of the painting. While the new painting has several aspects in common with the original Mona Lisa, there are also some significant differences. For instance, the subject has been changed to a male, and the painting has been given the name "The Mona Bob."

True or false? The young painter and The Mona Bob need to be concerned with copyright.

False.

All works, except for music, created before 1927 are in the public domain and are free for anyone to adapt, modify, and reuse without consent. And there's nothing the copyright owners or former copyright owners can do because their rights have expired.

Subscription Assets and Copyright

Milton has a subscription to Adobe Stock (https://stock.adobe.com), where he can access and download a vast collection of curated, royalty-free assets such as images and music files. Likewise, AJ has a subscription to Articulate 360 (https://articulate.com), where she can find millions of characters, videos, and images through Articulate's Content Library.

A common question subscribers ask is, "Can I use the subscription assets outside the vendor's tools."

For example, can AJ use a photo from Articulate's Content Library in her Microsoft PowerPoint presentation?

The answer: check the Terms of Service. The terms will likely prohibit AJ from using subscription assets outside the vendor's tools. The Terms of Service likely includes language that prevents her from using the subscription assets for new projects once the subscription has expired or is not renewed.

The following highlights some real-world copyright scenarios. Let's see if any of these result in copyright infringement.

Scenario 1: Bob teaching a colleague

Bob is teaching Sally how to deal with angry customers.

Bob is using PowerPoint as his presentation tool. He thinks it'll be a great idea to get an image of Mickey Mouse from the Internet and use it on some of his slides.

Bob's company is for-profit, but he's training a colleague. The course will never be seen by anyone outside of the company, nor will it be sold to customers.

Bob believes that using the Mickey Mouse image does not break copyright law because he only intends to use the image for internal training.

Is this okay?

Disney makes money by licensing its characters. Bob's use of the Mickey Mouse image sounds like the exact type of use that a license agreement from Disney would cover.

Bob is replacing the market value for Disney's image, and there would likely be a cause of action. Even though the image is used internally, the right to use the image is something that Bob's company should have purchased from Disney. By not purchasing a license to use the image, Bob's company is saving money and, therefore, seeing a financial benefit in its commercial endeavors.

Also, if Sally were to become disgruntled and report Bob, not only could Bob be held liable for the infringement, but so could the company.

Scenario 2: Joe the church volunteer

Joe is a church volunteer creating assets to support a fundraiser. Joe has included funny images of Bart Simpson in a document he created in Adobe InDesign.

Is that okay?

A church is considered a nonprofit organization. However, a fundraiser is regarded as a commercial venture. The use of the image would not be permitted.

Scenario 3: Sally and application training

Sally has been tasked with creating a training course to teach employees how to use Microsoft Word.

To create the training, Sally uses TechSmith SnagIt to make screen captures of the Word interface.

Is it okay for Sally to use the screen captures of Word in her training?

Because Sally is creating training material related to the program, it can be argued that it's a transformative use of the material that would be acceptable under fair use.

Scenario 4: Sam and the temporary download

Sam is teaching a class about images and editing them with Adobe Photoshop. She asks her entire class do a Google search, and they find a slice of pizza.

While the pizza image is protected by copyright, everyone downloads it to their computer, opens it with Photoshop, and edits it. Afterward, the image is deleted from every computer.

Is this okay?

Yes. The image wasn't used commercially, and it was discarded after use.

Copyright and Parodies

A parody has a specific meaning under copyright law. To be protected by the Constitution, a parody must take an image known or identifiable to its audience and then change it up in some way that makes a comment or a criticism on the subject matter.

The use will be defensible if you use only as much of the work needed to get your point across.

If, for example, you take a photo and combine it with something else to make it funny, the use will be less defensible.

Compelled to Break Copyright

A trainer was instructed to put several copyright-protected images into a corporate onboarding course.

Knowing the risk of infringement, the trainer refused to use the images. However, the boss insisted, and not wanting to rock the boat, the trainer relented.

As predicted, the copyright owner sued. Who is going to pay for the copyright infringement? The trainer? The boss? The company?

In this instance, all three parties could be liable.

The trainer is responsible as a direct infringer. The boss is a contributory infringer who induced the trainer to do the infringing act. And the company benefited from the infringement.

Any of the three parties could end up paying the whole amount, or the fine could be split among the parties however they want.

Internet Search Images and Copyright

Suppose you would like to use an image of a puppy in your training to add a touch of "cute." It's simple to search the Internet for "puppy," just click the Images tab, and download from a nearly unlimited number of choices. In the image below, you can see that choices abound.

Figure 11: An Internet search for puppies.

While it's tempting to use these images in your training document, presentation, or eLearning project, you should assume that all of the images are protected by copyright.

There is a way to find images through an Internet search and avoid copyright infringement.

Using your web browser, search for Google Advanced Search and click the Advanced Search link.

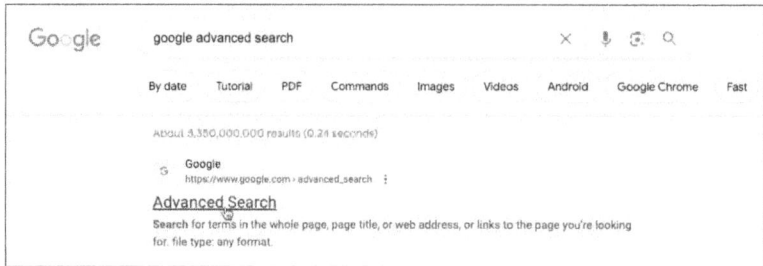

Figure 12: Google advanced search.

In the box labeled **all these words**, type puppy.

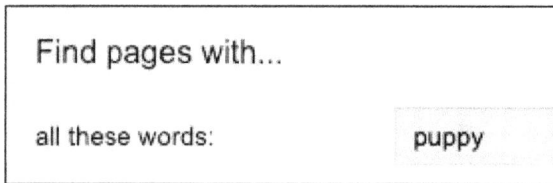

Figure 13: Fill pages with all these words.

At the bottom of the Search window is an area called **usage rights**.

From the drop-down menu, choose free to use, share or modify, even commercially.

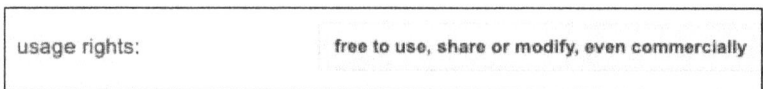

Figure 14: Usage rights.

After clicking the **Advanced Search** button, images that meet your search criteria are shown. While there aren't as many puppy images as before, there is still a vast selection from which to choose.

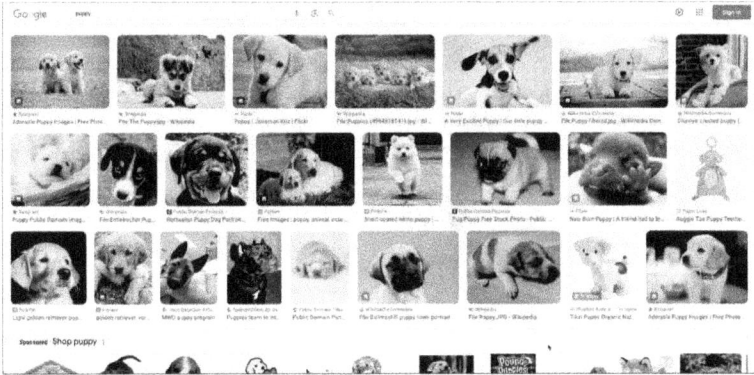

Figure 15: Images that are free to use, share or modify, even commercially.

The search results look promising. However, you must check the license terms and ensure you can use the image.

For example, the trainer would like to use the image shown below.

Figure 16: Puppy image found via an Internet search.

Clicking the image and visiting the website that hosts the image opens a page that usually includes an area covering licensing.

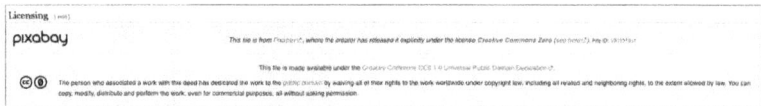

Figure 17: Information about licensing the puppy image.

The licensing text for this particular image says, "This file is from Pixabay.com, where the creator has released it explicitly under the license Creative Commons Zero (also known as CC Zero or CC0)."

According to creativecommons.org, CC0 "is a public dedication tool, which enables creators to give up their copyright and put their works into the worldwide public domain. CC0 enables reusers to distribute, remix, adapt, and build upon the material in any medium or format, with no conditions."

In short, you can use the image above in your training without fear of breaking copyright law.

When reviewing licensing agreements, you might also see a message that says you are free to use the image, but you must give attribution.

For example, some license agreements say: "You must give appropriate credit, provide a link to the license, and indicate if changes were made. You may do so in any *reasonable* manner, but not in any way that suggests the license holder endorses you or your use."

The word "reasonable" is open to interpretation. What is reasonable to one person might not be reasonable to another person.

Copyright Infringement as a Business Model

A poem found while searching the Internet offers the perfect motivation that a trainer would like to include in his course.

He innocently copies a few lines from the poem and pastes it onto his PowerPoint slide.

Later, upon completing the course, he uploads it to his Learning Management System and moves on.

A few months later, he receives a letter from a lawyer that warns the trainer to stop using the poem. The letter says something to the effect that "Normally, the fine for using our poem without permission is $100,000. Because this is the first time we've noticed you've violated our copyright, we'll be nice and offer you a settlement of $6,000 if you pay it by Tuesday."

The trainer contacted a lawyer who confirmed that the letter was authentic, and that the poem content needed to be removed from the training immediately.

The lawyer also advised that the potential fine was accurate. The proposed settlement was considered a bargain.

The trainer took the lawyer's advice. She modified the course by removing the poem's content, paid the fine, and considered herself lucky her mistake didn't cost more.

This true-life scenario is an example of copyright holders using their rights to make money.

If you have registered the copyright, you can find infringers and take them to court for violating your copyright. Finding copyright infringers can be very lucrative.

One of the first things that a copyright holder will do is send a cease-and-desist letter like the trainer in the example. Instead of going through litigation, which the copyright owner would probably win, the infringer will be asked to settle out of court.

Settling out of court could be a wise business decision. If you have indeed broken copyright law, you will lose the case. You may also be required to pay a substantial fine and attorney's fees.

The author of the poem mentioned in the example eventually sold the right to collect copyright infringement damages to a collection company. We call these companies copyright trolls because their business model is based on finding infringers and extracting fees. While it's not a pleasant business model for people who innocently violate copyright law, it's perfectly legal.

Another common trolling practice is to upload an image to Google and perform a reverse image lookup.

If you click the **Search by image** icon on Google, the screen shown in the second image below will pop up:

Figure 18: Search by image icon.

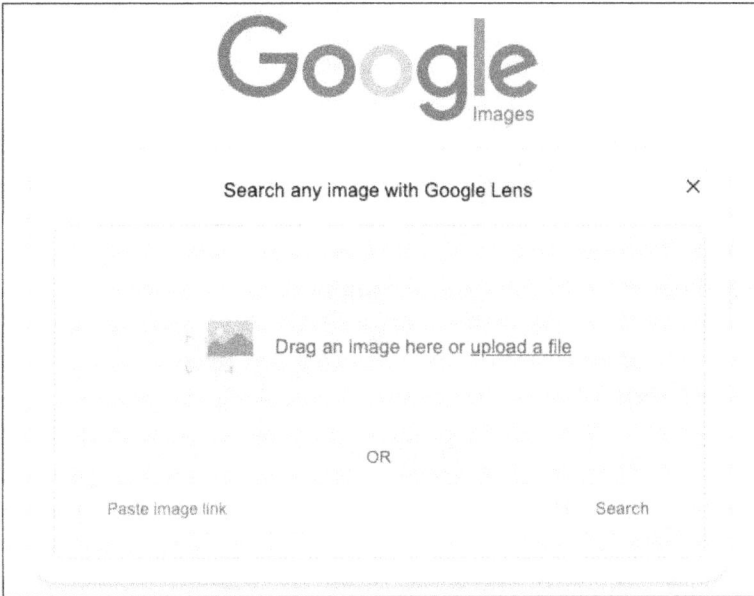

Figure 19: Search any image with Google Lens screen.

In the example below, the puppy image was uploaded. Within seconds, websites using the image are displayed.

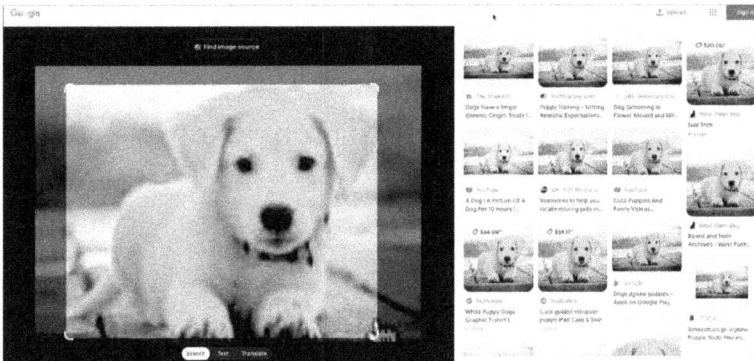

Figure 20: Puppy image uploaded.

The example puppy image is free to use, but what if an image is protected by copyright? Anyone can contact the copyright holder and say, "Hey, just so you know, I discovered that your image is being used illegally. I see that you own the copyright. If you share the wealth with me, I'll tell you who is using it."

It's a good bet that the copyright holder would elect to work with this individual and share the revenue from either a settlement or lawsuit.

To get around copyright restrictions for videos found on YouTube, eLearning developers can embed a link to the YouTube video instead of importing the video into the project.

In most instances, this approach will not break copyright law because you are not hosting the video yourself. You are only providing a link for people to view the posted video on YouTube.

Copyright Fines

If a copyright was registered before the infringement, the owner can ask for up to $30,000 in damages, even if the person who used the copyrighted work never made any money.

If a copyright notice was added to the work and it was registered, the owner can ask for up to $150,000.

If the case goes to court and the owner wins, the person who committed the infringement will have to pay the fine and all attorney's fees.

Creative Commons

Creative Commons is a platform that was invented to streamline the permissions process. Authors can put their work on Creative Commons by giving it a license attribution.

There are six licenses under the Creative Commons model. They are listed below, including if the license allows for commercial use. (Addendum: Commercial is not something where you make money. Something is only considered commercial if you are attempting to make money or promote or advertise something, such as a product, a service, or a cause.)

- **CC BY**: Allows for commercial use. Reusers can distribute, remix, adapt, and build upon the material in any medium or format, so long as attribution is credited to the creator.

- **CC By-SA**: Allows for commercial use. Requires attribution, and if you mix, adapt, or build on the material, you must license your version of the work to other users under identical terms.

- **CC By-NC**: Noncommercial use only. Reusers can distribute, remix, adapt, and build upon the material in any medium or format, so long as attribution is credited to the creator.

- **CC By-NC-SA**: Noncommercial use only. Reusers can distribute, remix, adapt, and build upon the material in any medium or format, and only so long as attribution is credited to the creator. If you remix, adapt, or build upon the material, you must license the modified material under identical terms.

- **CC BY-ND**: Allows for commercial use. Reusers can copy and distribute the material in any medium or format in unadapted form only so long as attribution is credited to the creator.

- **CC BY-NC-ND**: Noncommercial use only. Reusers can copy and distribute the material in any medium or format in unadapted form only, so long as attribution is credited to the creator.

(**Source**: https://creativecommons.org/share-your-work/cclicenses.)

Copyright Reuse Strategies

If you would like to use copyrighted work in your training, there are some steps you can take to ensure you have permission to use the assets.

Read the Fine Print

Visit the website hosting the copyrighted work. Review the Terms of Use. As you review the Terms of Use, remember that the language used in the agreements can be verbose and difficult to understand. While some believe the language is intentionally written to be challenging to understand, that is not necessarily the case.

Lawyers have not teamed up and agreed to make the vocabulary as hard to read as possible. It's more likely that the agreement language was kept broad to apply to all anticipated uses.

Visit the Copyright Office

The copyright office maintains a database of works created in 1976 and later (https://www.copyright.gov/public-records/). This database will allow you to conduct keyword searches to determine who the authors are. Once you find out the names of the author(s), you can contact them to seek permission to use the work.

As mentioned earlier in this book, if you want to reuse copyrighted music, you can search the Songfile database (https://www.songfile.com).

Remember that, especially with music, there can be multiple copyright owners. To be safe, get permission from all owners before reusing the work.

Just because a work you found through your research on the Internet doesn't mention anything regarding copyright, that does not mean you are free and clear to use it. As mentioned at the beginning of this book, the owner of a work does not have to file for a copyright, and the work does not have to be registered.

If the work isn't yours, and you cannot find the owner, the best course is **not to use the work**.

Trust But Verify

You've inherited a training presentation and have been tasked with updating it. There is media used throughout the course that are concerning. For instance, where did your predecessor get the images?

Colleagues, perhaps even your boss, assure you that the images aren't a copyright concern.

Verifying that the images are safe to use can put you in an uncomfortable position. Still, you'll be a hero in your organization if you find even a single image that breaks copyright law.

Sure, you can bury your head in the sand, use the images, and hope for the best. After all, if you or your organization get sued, you can always ask for forgiveness, right?

Even a single violation puts you at the mercy of the copyright owner, and you don't know what position they will take.

Consider the high school coach who posted an excerpt from a motivational book he was reading on his social media. The copyright holder sued the teacher and the school for $150,000.

The court decided that there was neither a commercial benefit, nor a commercial purpose in the posting of these motivational pieces. Therefore, there was no liability. But it could have easily gone the other way.

While the court sided with the coach and the school, both parties still had to defend themselves. There were substantial legal fees, mental anguish, and distraction from work and family life. Litigating is not pleasant.

Here's another example: A singer wanted to perform a cover song using a part of somebody else's song and somebody else's music.

The singer started negotiating with the music's copyright owner, but the negotiations broke down. The singer who wanted to reuse and remake the music made a demo that they sent to the original copyright saying, "Here's how we want to use it. Take a look at this. Will you let us do it?"

Somebody released and leaked the demo, and the copyright owner sued.

You Never Know Until You Ask

Getting permission to use copyrighted content can be a straightforward process. It's just a matter of setting up good business practices to ensure you have permission to use the asset the way you want.

A musician wanted to use copyrighted artwork on the cover of a CD.

The musician contacted the artist by email and asked to use the artwork. The artist said, "Sure. It's fine."

It took a few days, but the musician got a contract and license agreement from the artist. The musician can now legally use the artwork.

Add a Clause to Your Development Contract

If you're an eLearning developer hired to create a course, the client will likely provide some media for you to use as you build the course.

The agreement made between you and the client should state that for any images provided by the client, the client agrees that appropriate usage permissions have been obtained.

The contract should also include language such as: *If any of the promises that you made in this contract, including our ability to reuse any intellectual property that was given to us, results in a lawsuit, you agree to pay all of our legal costs and the damages.*

Copyright Insurance

They say there's an insurance policy for everything. And, yes, copyright insurance exists. You can purchase advertising injury insurance covering your use of images, should you be subjected to a copyright lawsuit.

A quick search on the Internet will help you to locate several agencies that provide copyright insurance. Typical insurance policies limit your liability, while the insurer pays the rest.

According to Insureon (https://www.insureon.com), an agency that provides small business insurance, "Being on the wrong side of a copyright infringement lawsuit could cost your small business thousands of dollars in legal fees, rebranding expenses, and confiscated materials.

"Fortunately, your general liability insurance policy will likely cover your expenses if another company accuses you of stepping too close to their trademarked name, branding, or products."

Negotiate

Chester Karass has written multiple books on the subject of negotiating, such as *The Negotiating Game: How to Get What You Want* and *In Business as in Life, You Don't Get What You Deserve, You Get What You Negotiate.*

That second book's title says it all: "You don't get what you deserve; you get what you negotiate."

The idea behind the saying is that you can often negotiate with the copyright holder. Discuss and let the copyright holder know you made a mistake. Let them know that you removed the asset from your website. Discuss the fine.

What you don't want to do is sound aggressive. Saying, "I'm not going to pay anything. We'll see you in court," is wrong. You're not going to intimidate anyone, and you're likely going to lose the case.

While every situation differs, your ability to negotiate with the copyright holder depends on their objectives. Remember, for some people, copyright infringement is a business model. They make their living on finding violators and settling out of court.

Nevertheless, it never hurts to talk and inquire. One strategy involves turning the fee into a license fee and saying, "You're asking me for $6,000 on Tuesday to settle this out of court. What if I pay you $6,500, and we can still use your image?"

That's a Wrap!

Thank you for taking the time to read or listen to this book.

During this book, we provided an easy-to-understand, straightforward overview and scenarios of typical copyright concerns seen by trainers, presenters, and eLearning content creators.

You've learned about the following copyright concepts:

- What is copyright?

- Works that are considered authored

- Originality

- How long does a copyright last?

- What rights do you get with a copyright?

- Is it necessary to file for a copyright?

- Artificial intelligence and copyright

- Sharing copyright

- Copyright roles

- Filing for a copyright

- Fair Use

- Audio use strategies

- Derivative works

- Subscription assets and copyright

- Copyright and parodies

- Being compelled to break copyright

- Internet search images and copyright

- Copyright infringement as a business model

- Copyright fines

- Creative commons

- Copyright reuse strategies

- Copyright insurance

- Negotiating

Copyright law can be complex. If you are concerned about your right to use an asset in your training, proceed cautiously.

Don't use the asset without ensuring you have the right to do so.

Consult with a legal professional, perform research, and document your findings. Your due diligence can and will pay off should you find yourself in a legal battle and facing a fine.

www.ingramcontent.com/pod-product-compliance
Lightning Source LLC
Chambersburg PA
CBHW060643210326
41520CB00010B/1715